Copyright © 2020 Joshua Stevens

All rights reserved. No part of this book may be reproduced or used in any manner without written permission of the copyright owner except for the use of quotations in a book review.
For more information: howtodrawanimalsgood@gmail.com

First Edition: February 2020

ISBN-13: 9798601458337

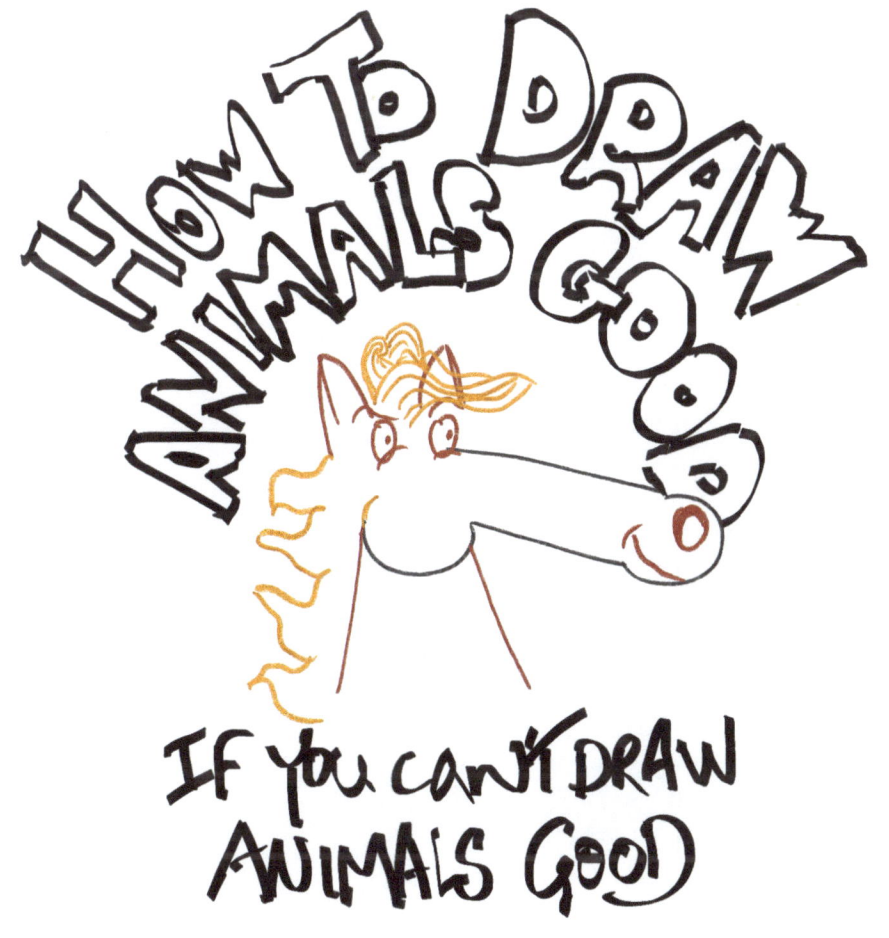

By Joshua Stevens.

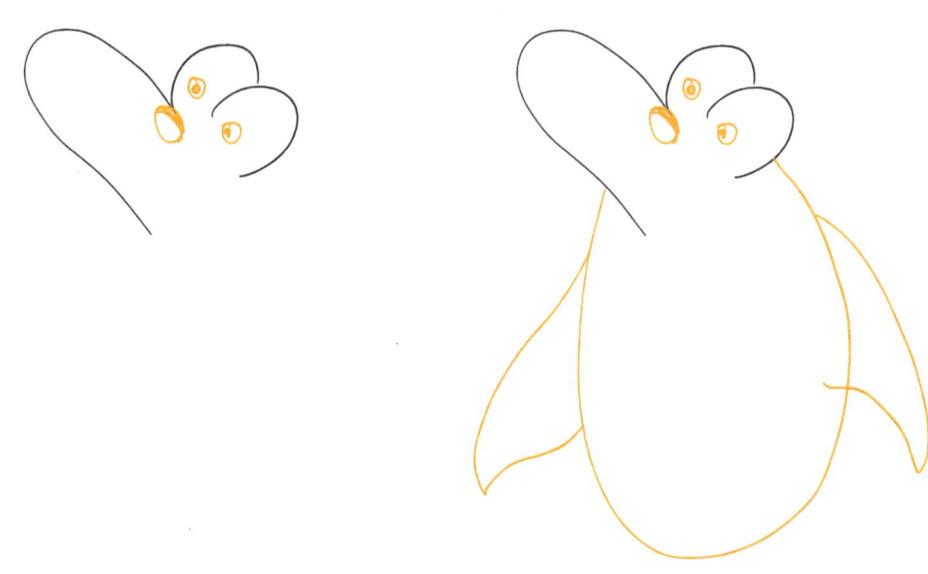
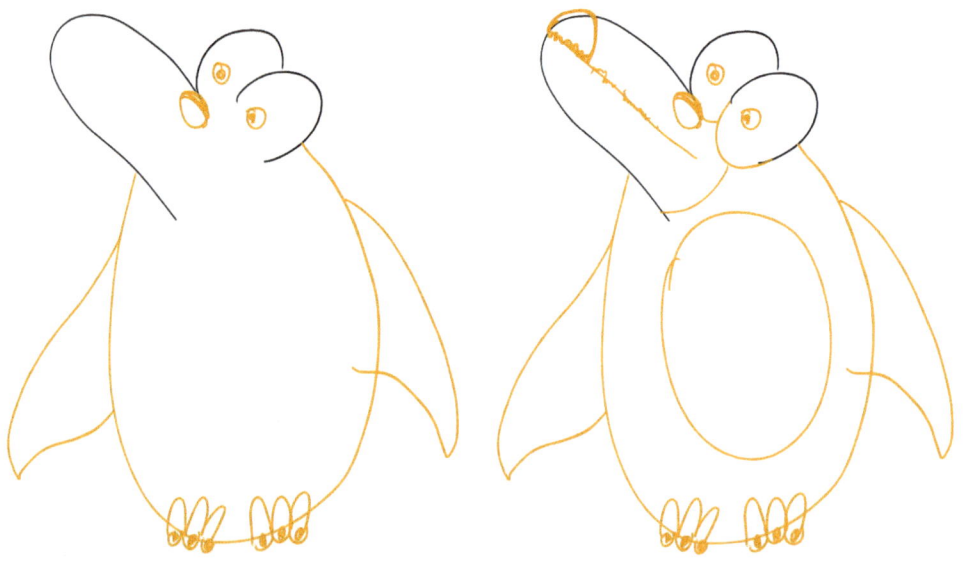

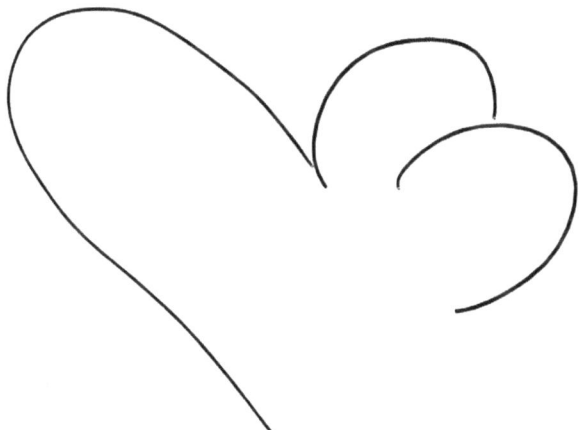

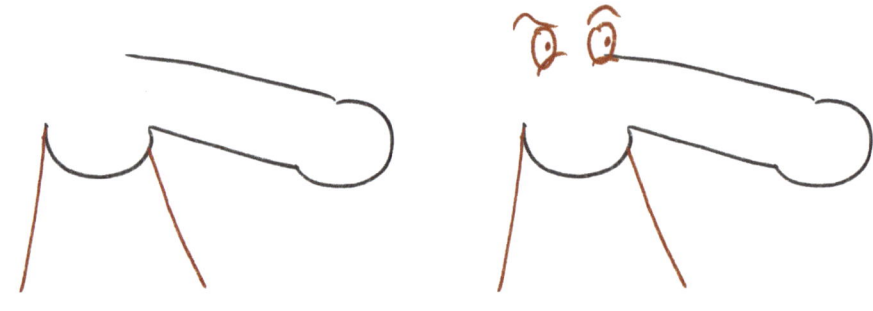
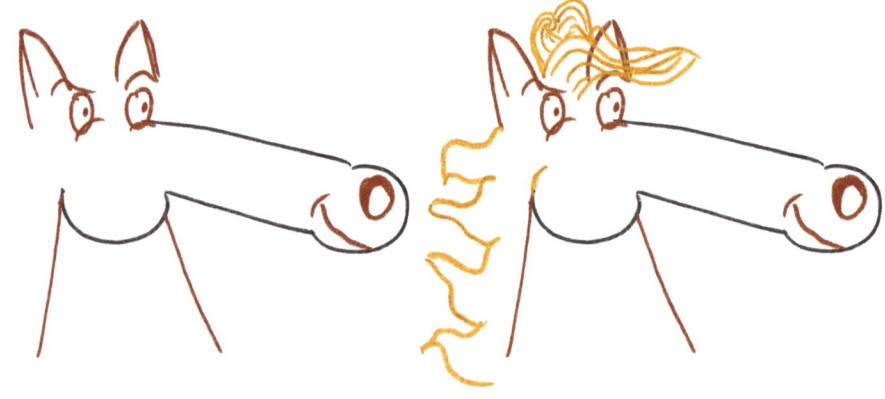

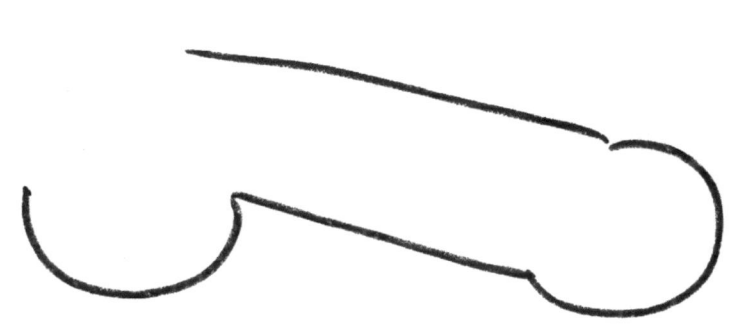

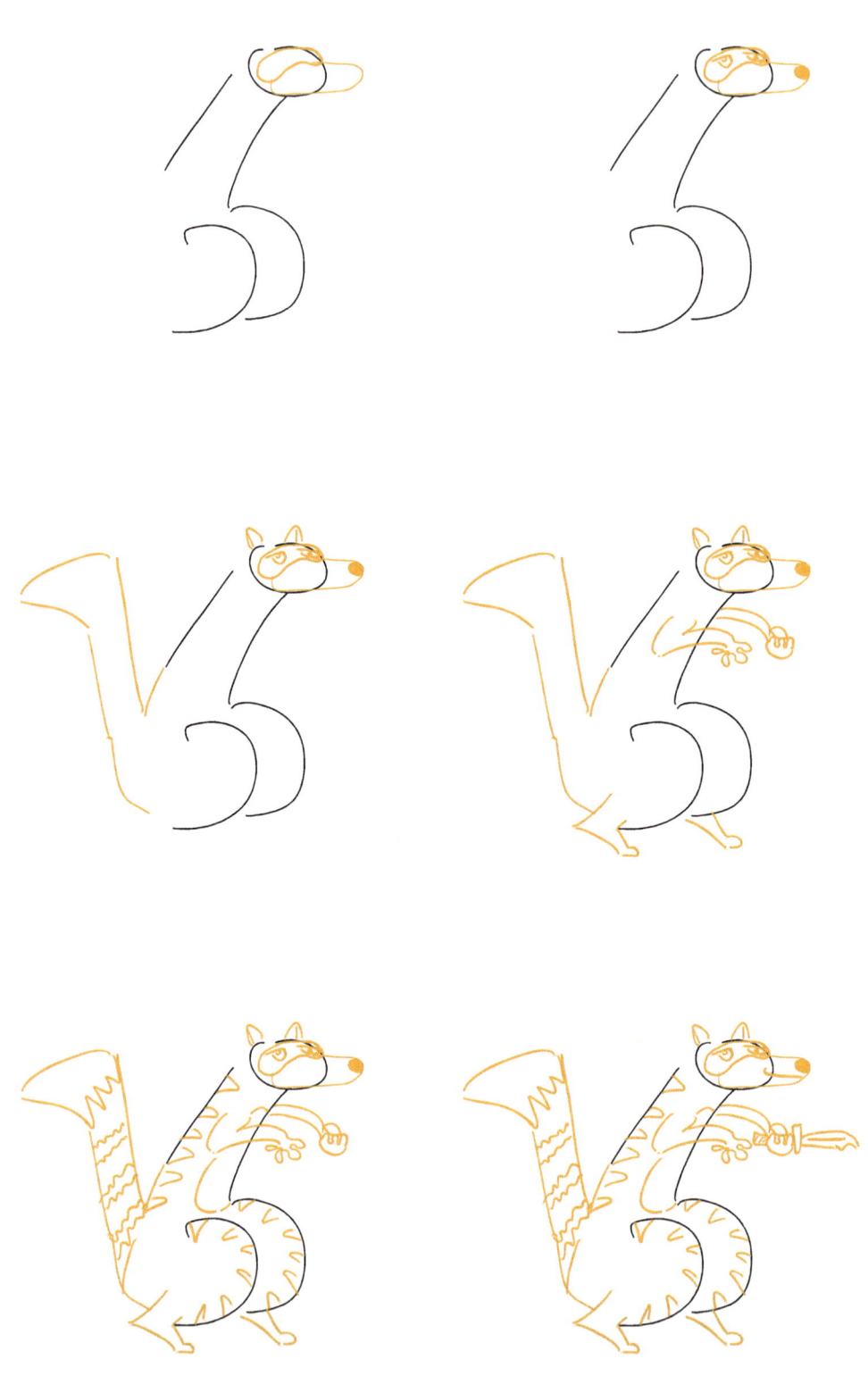

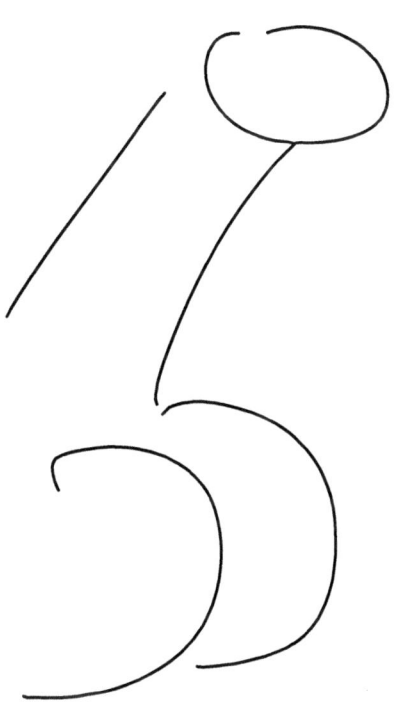

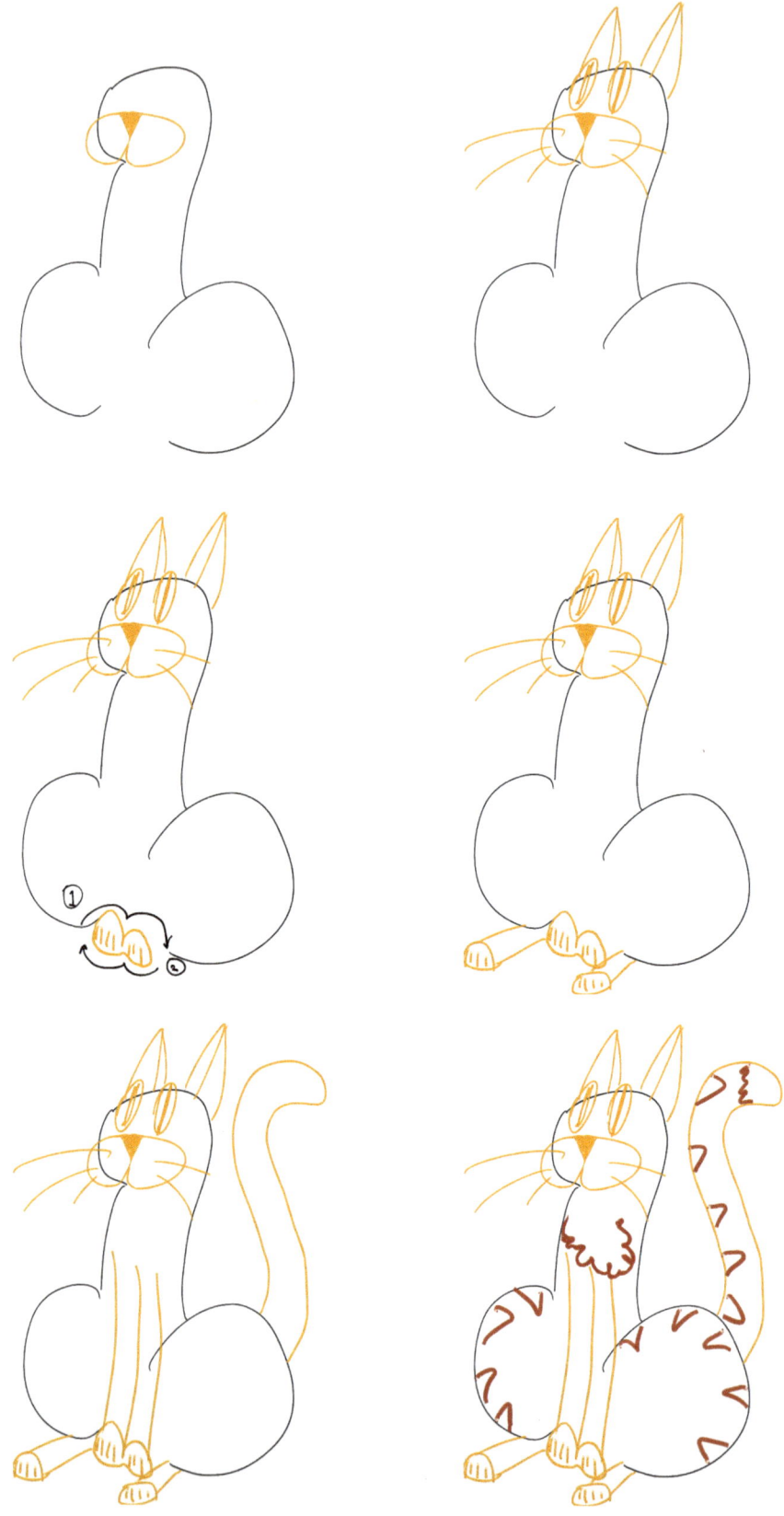

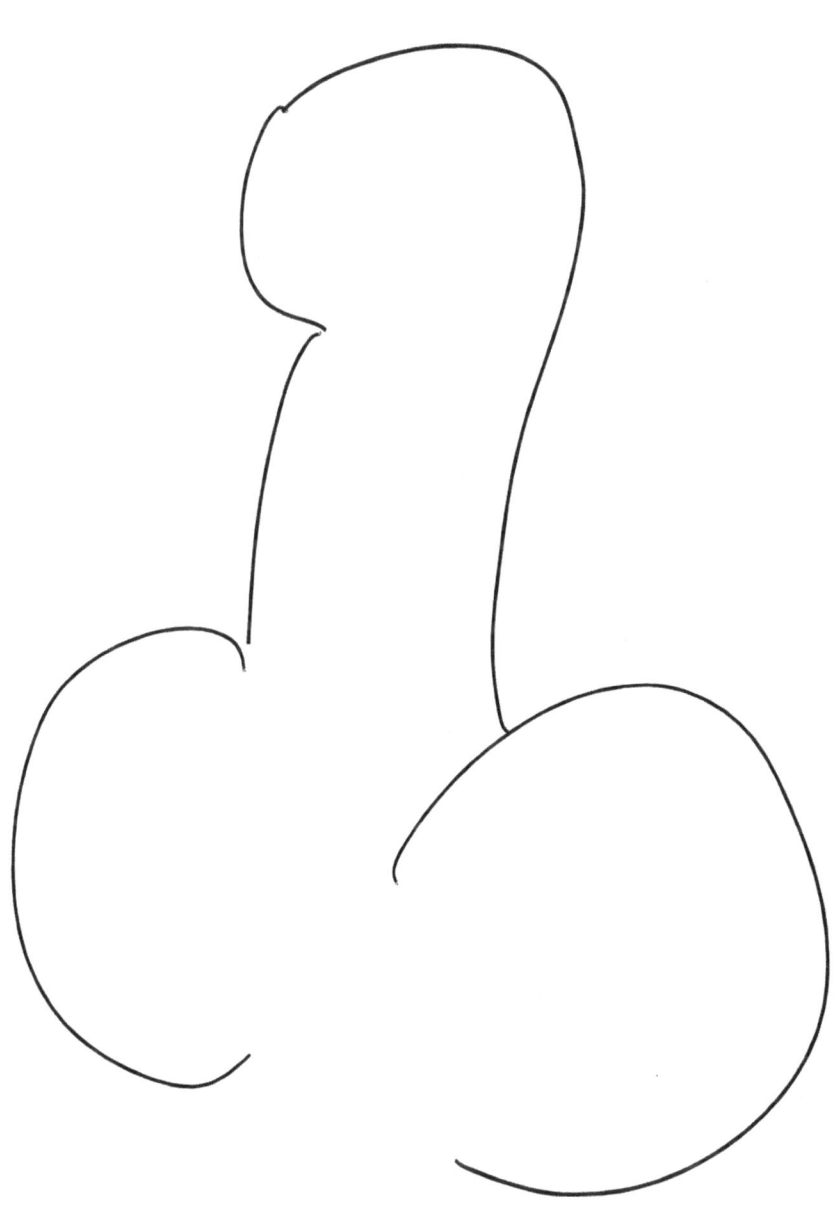

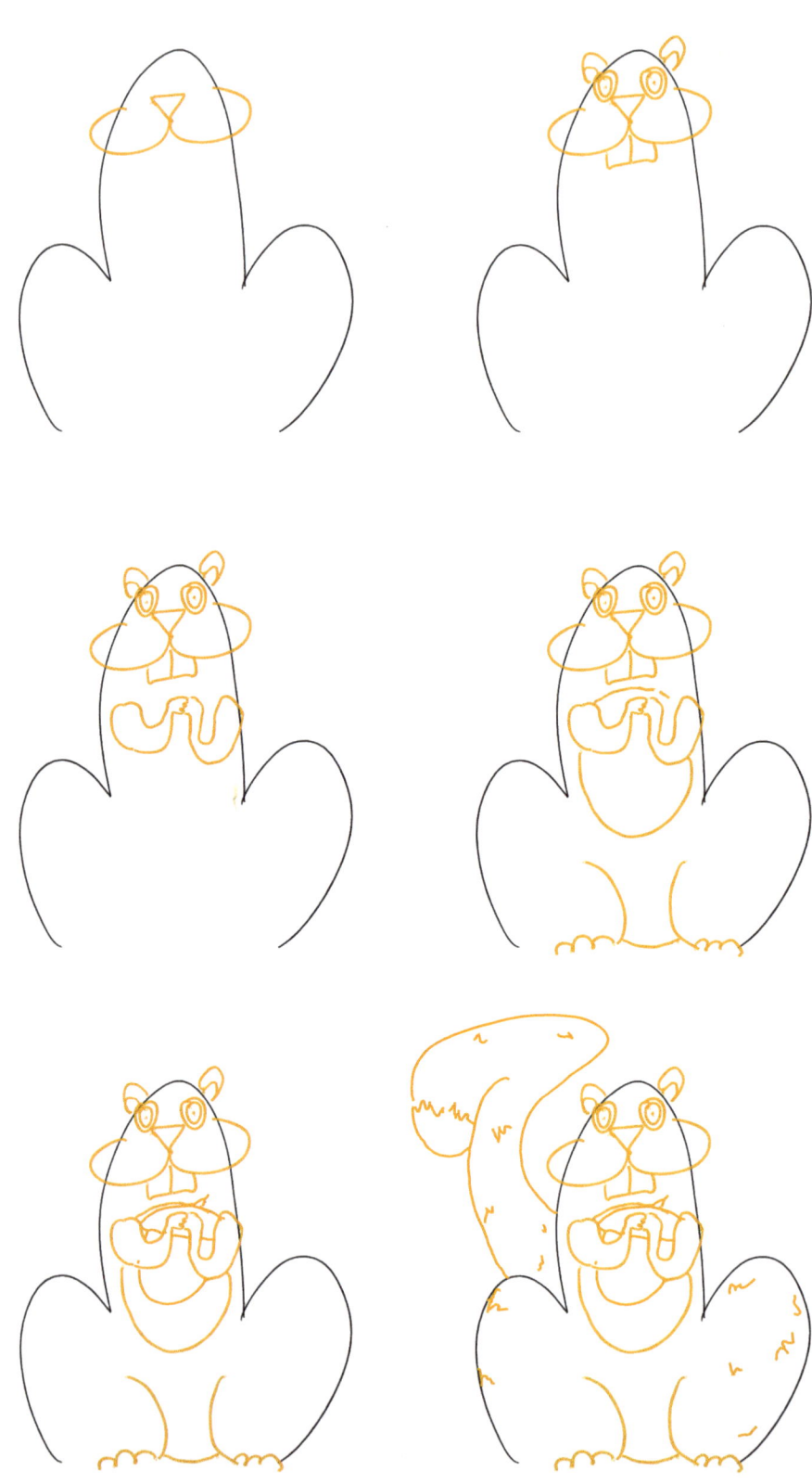

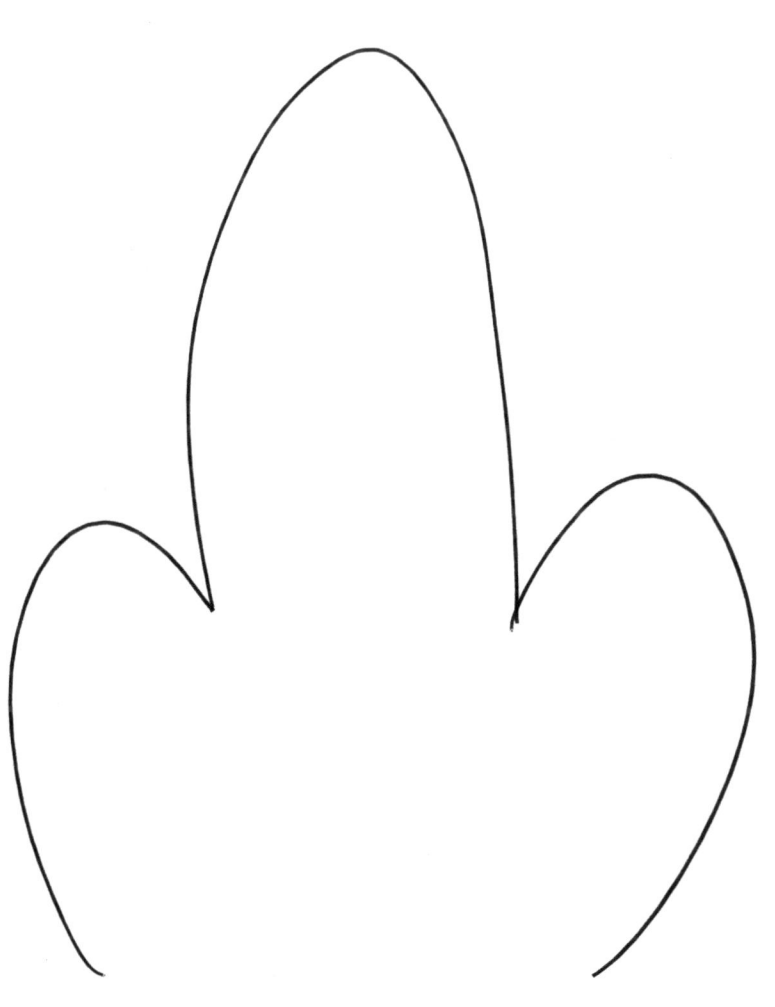

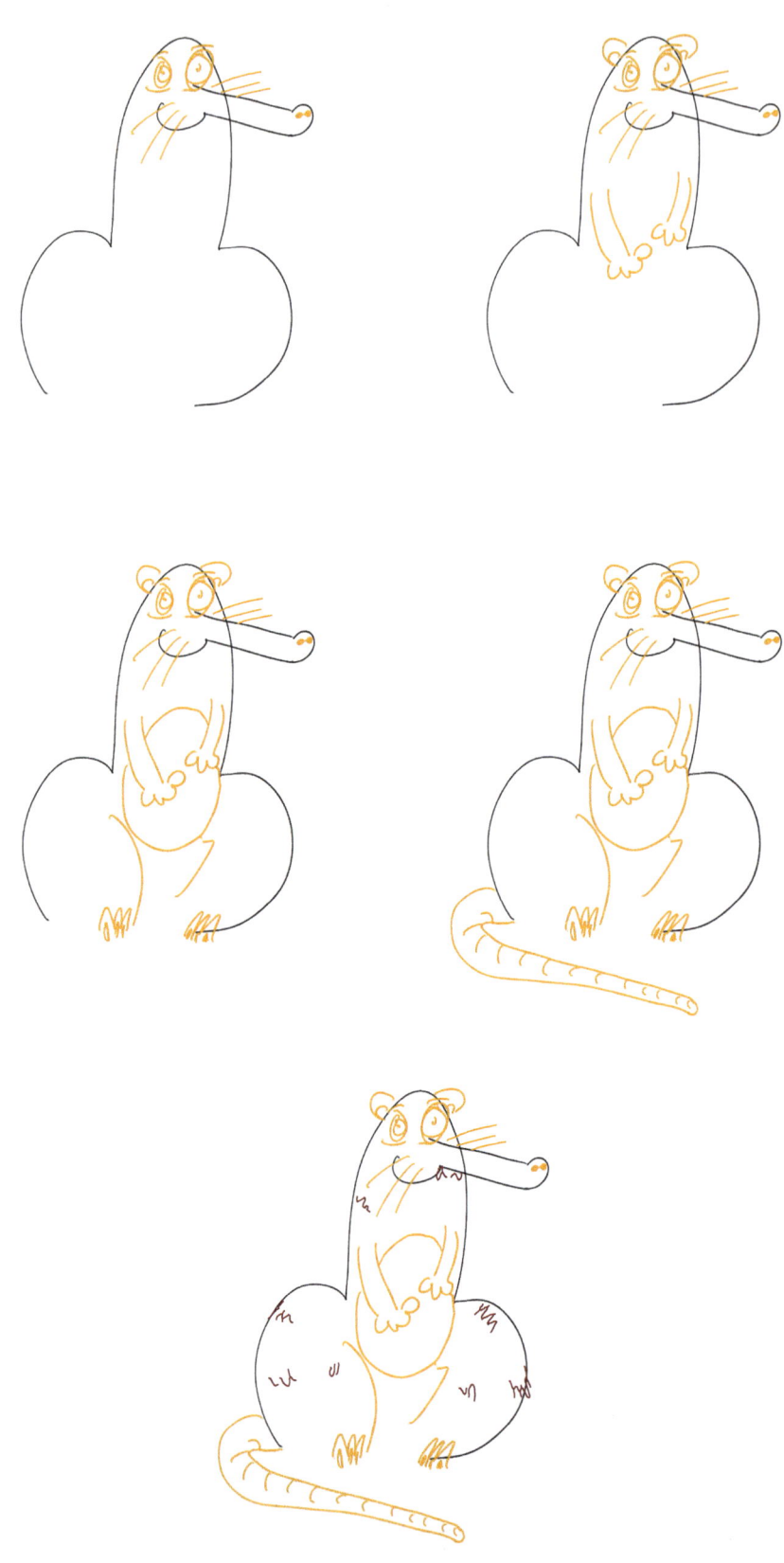

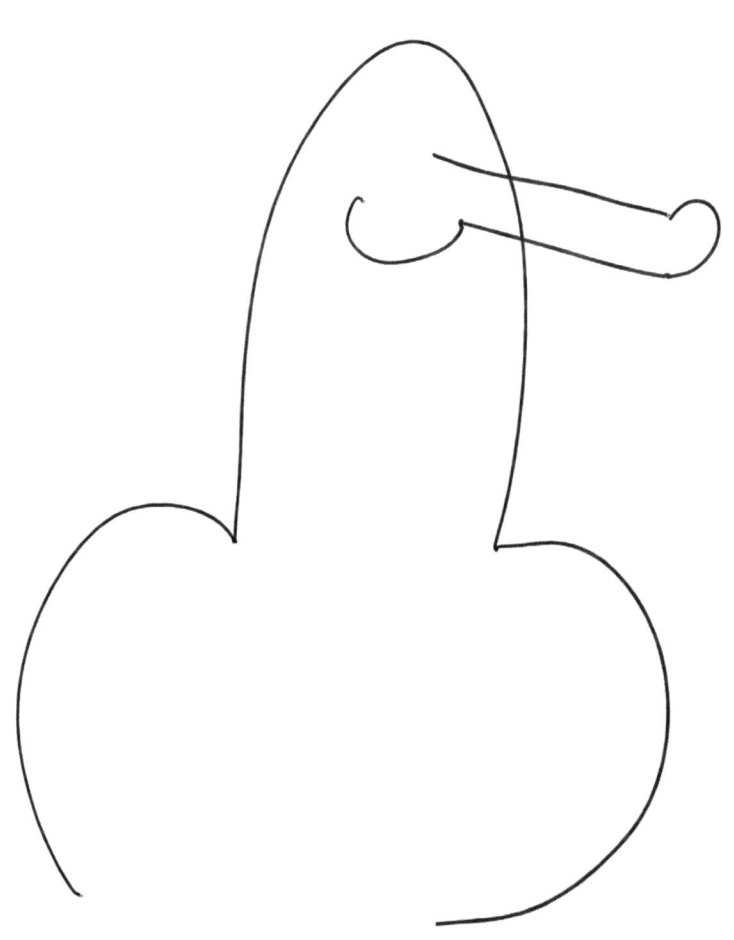

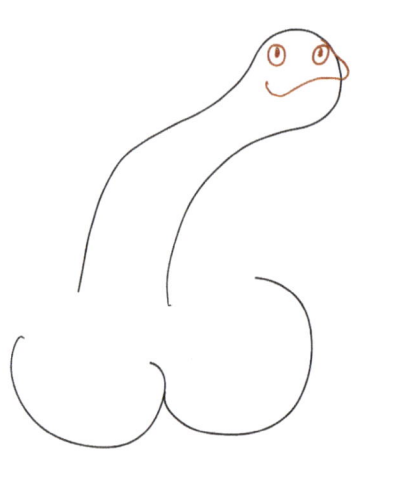 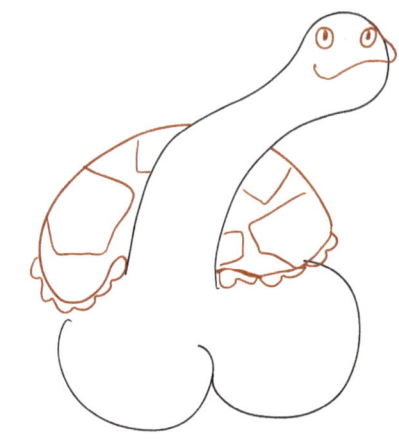
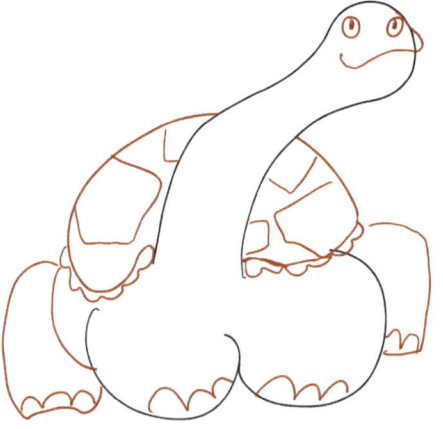 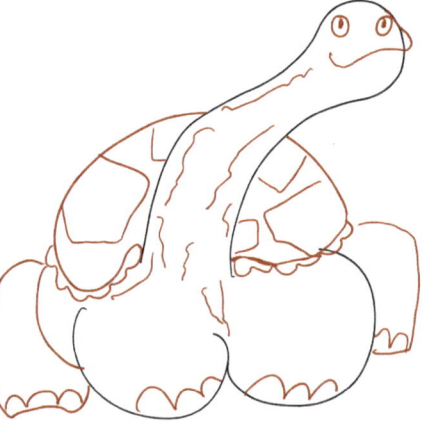

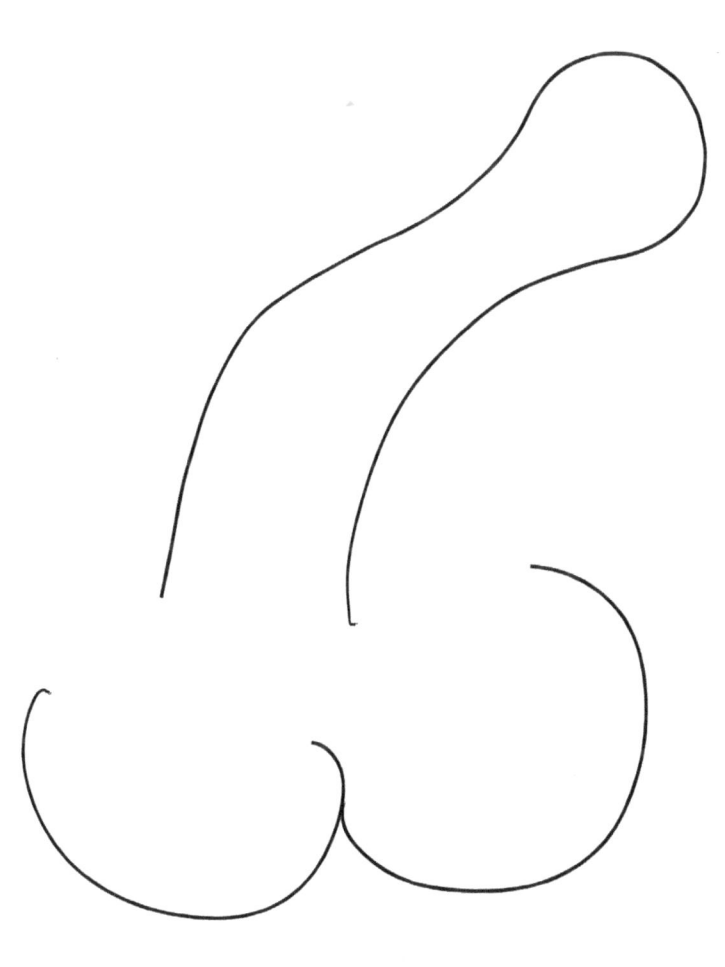

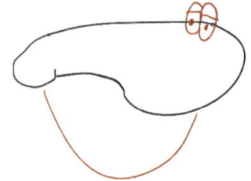
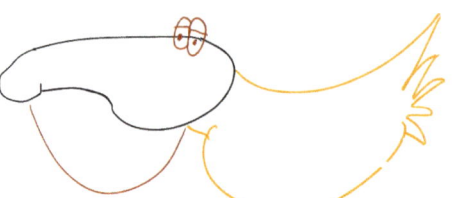
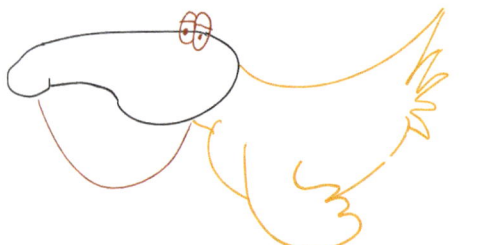
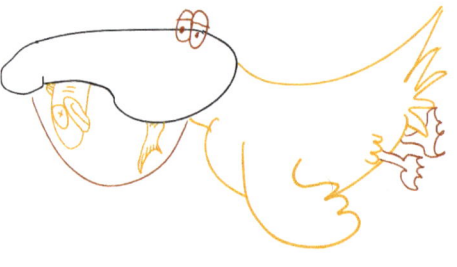

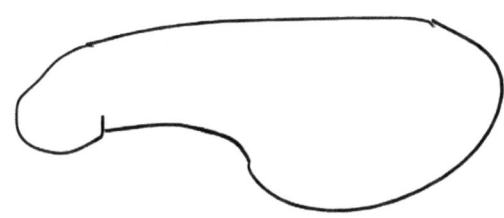

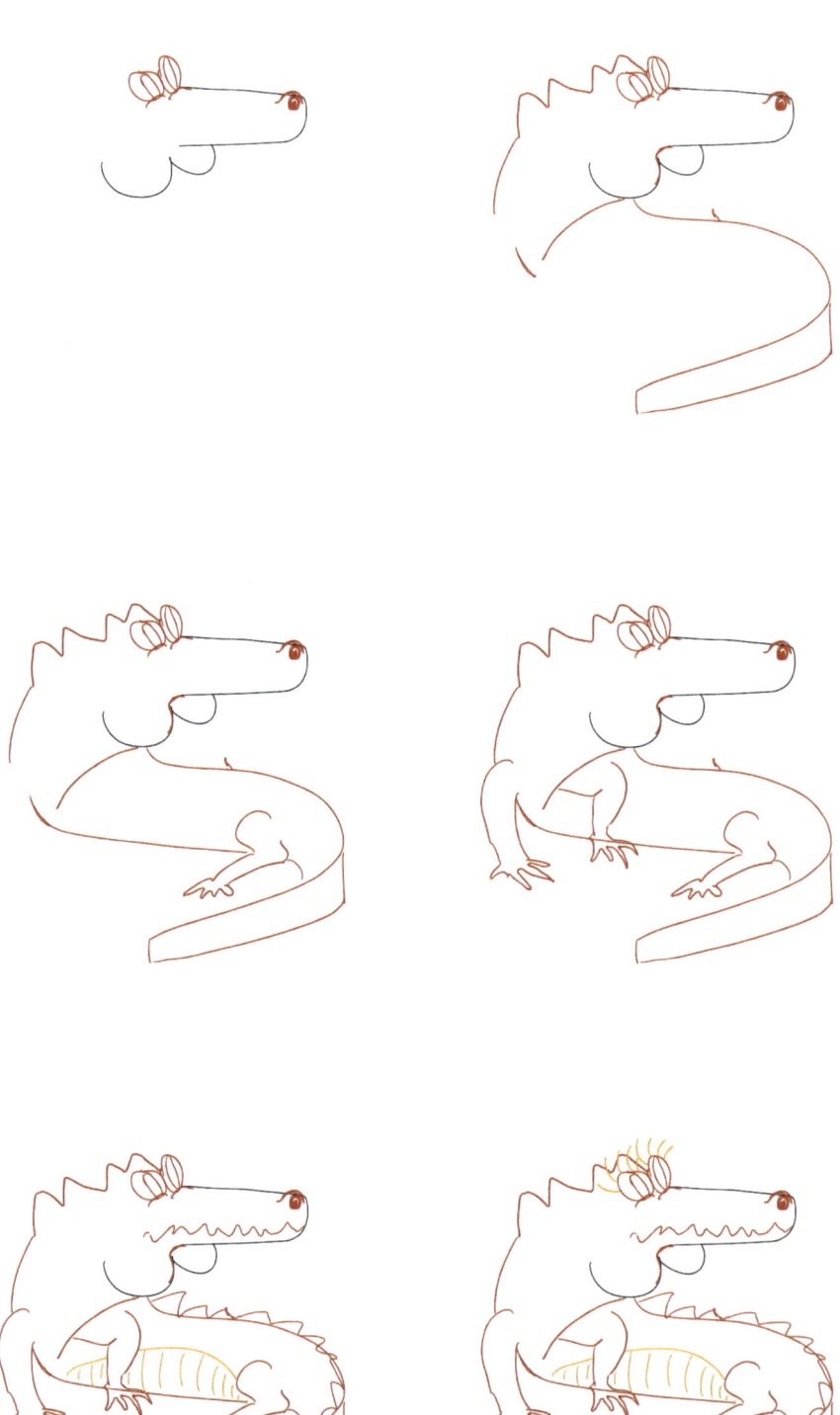

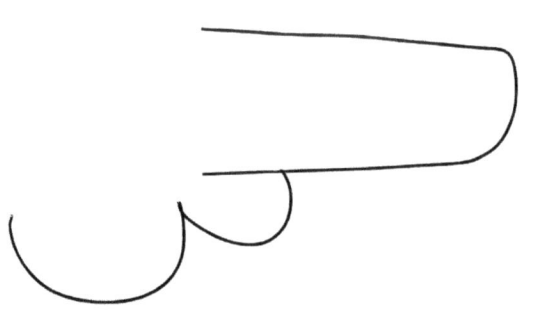

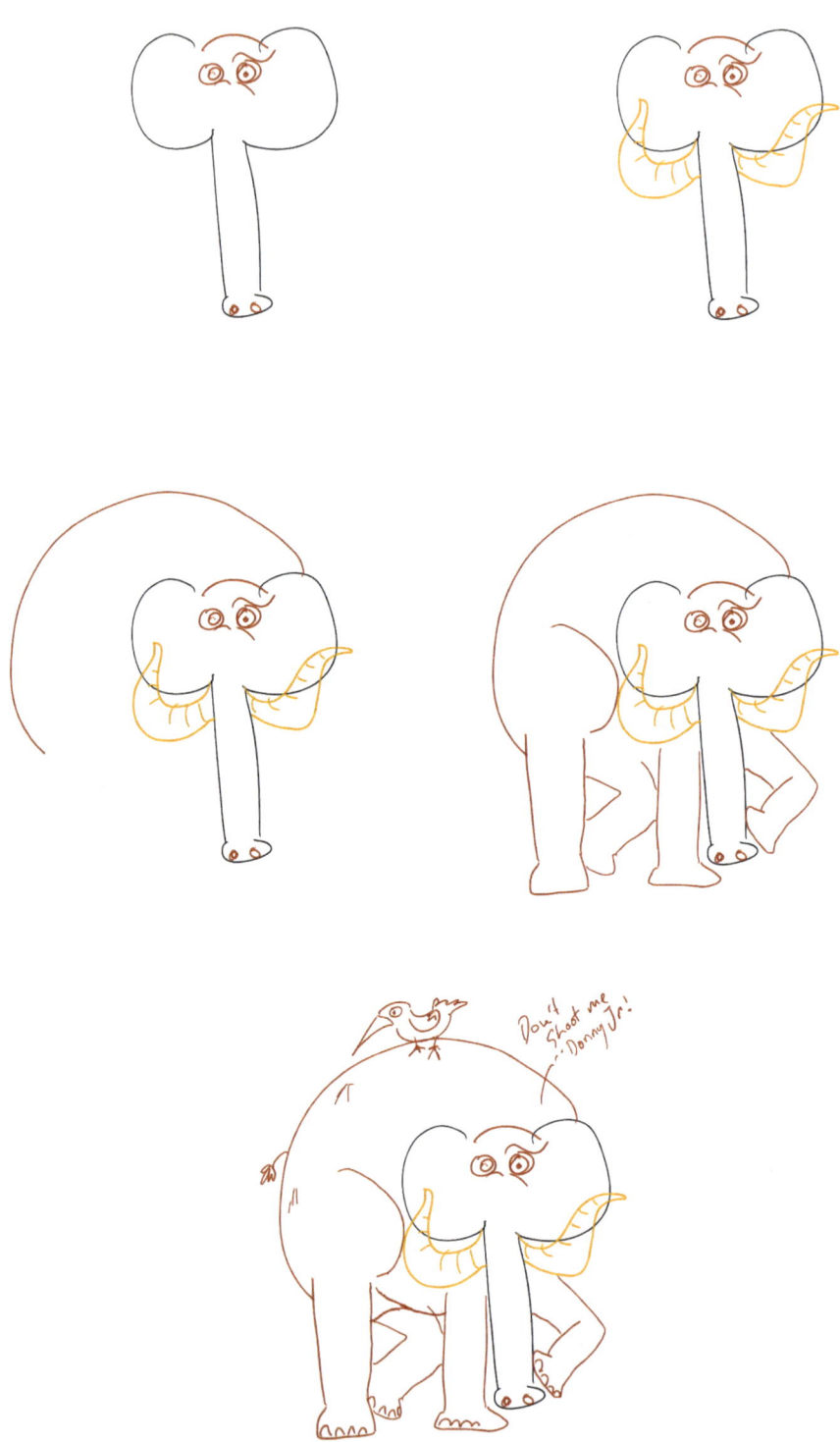

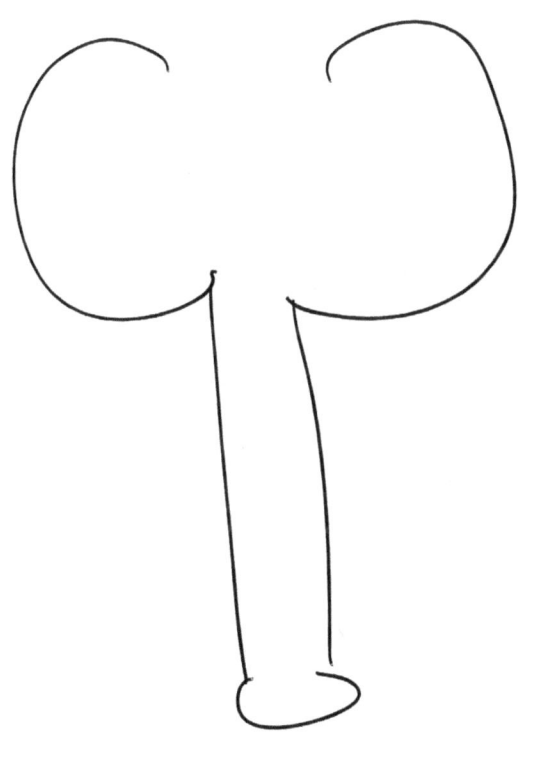

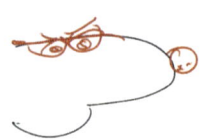
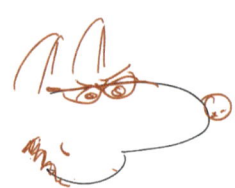
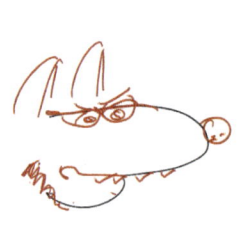
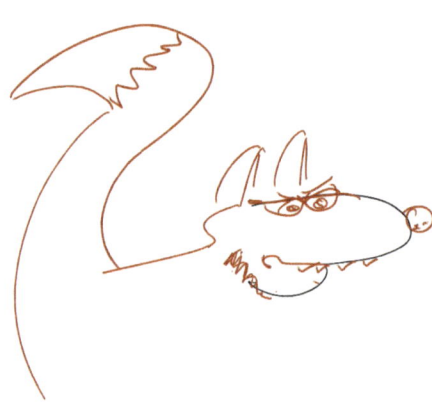
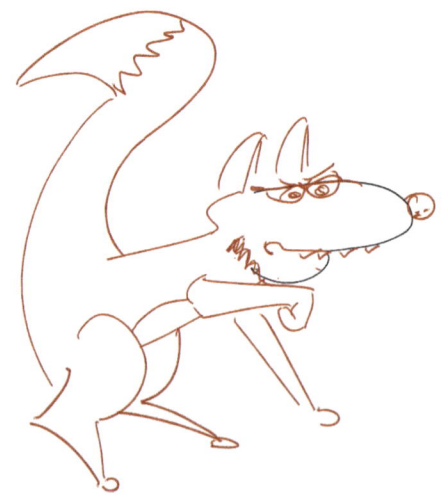
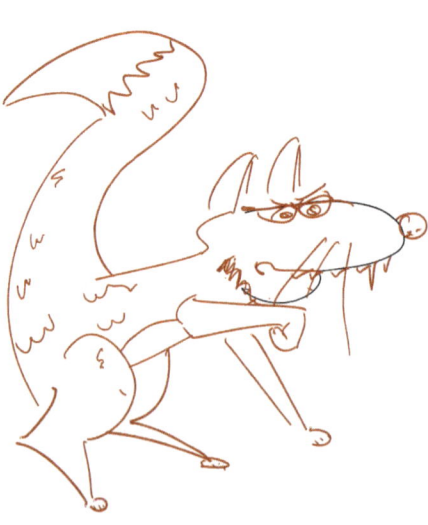

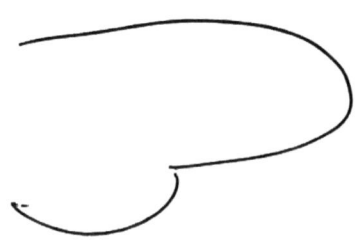

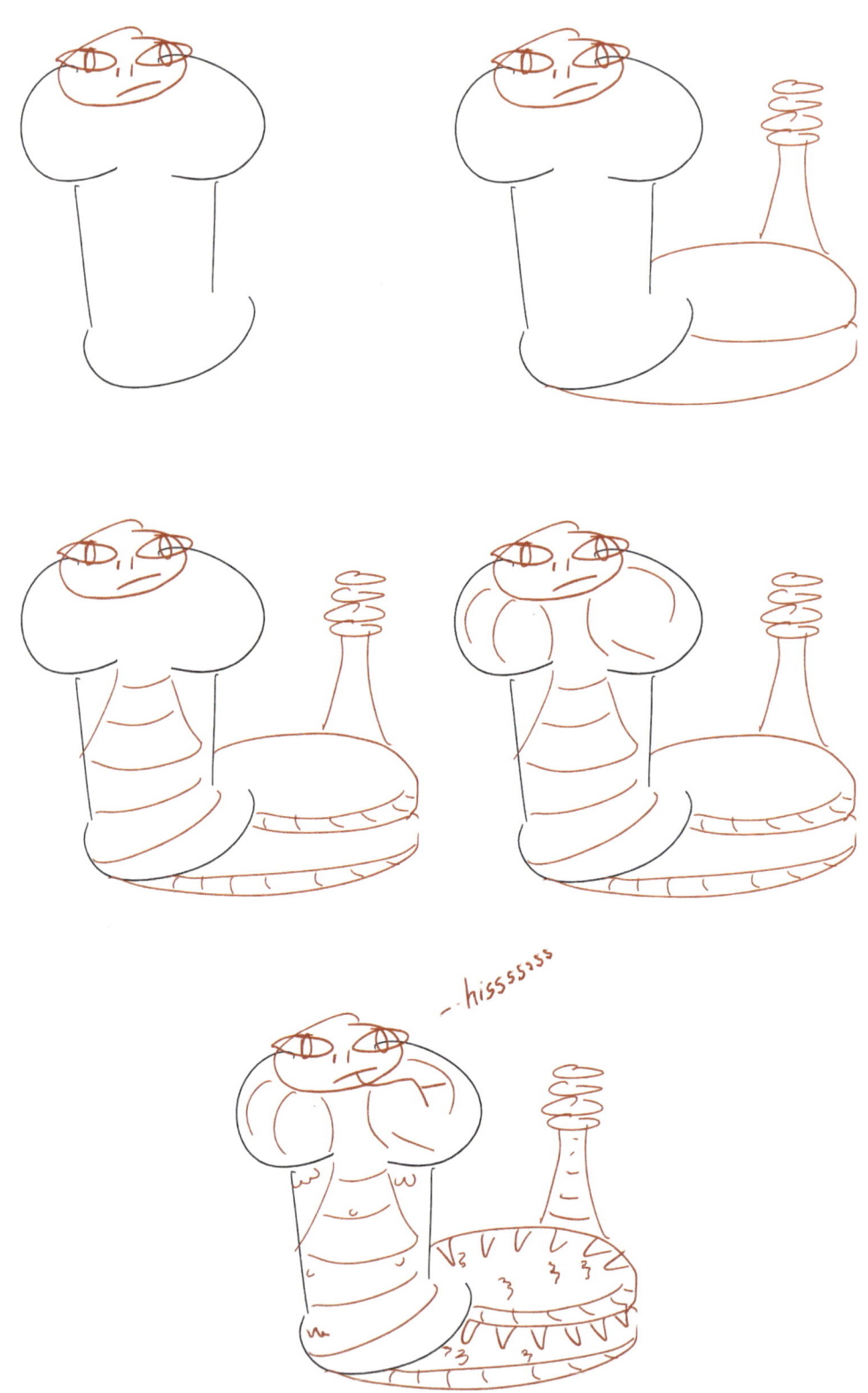

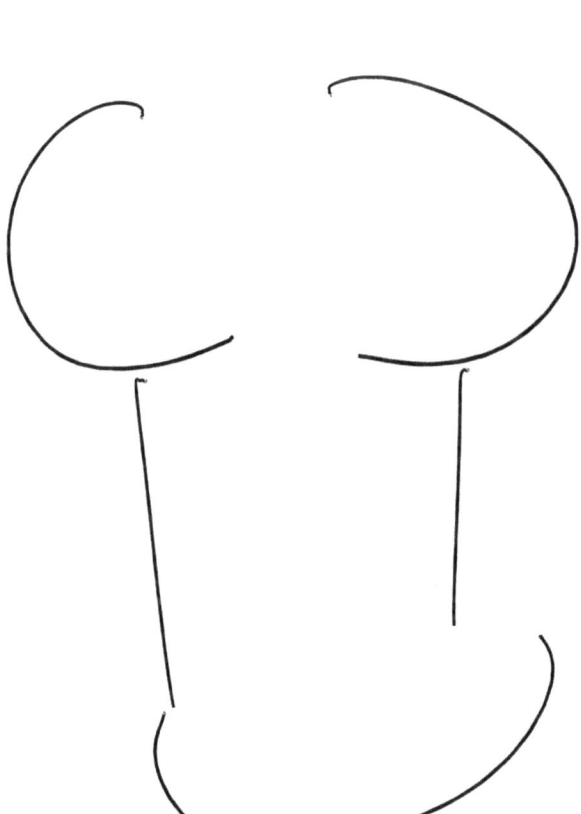

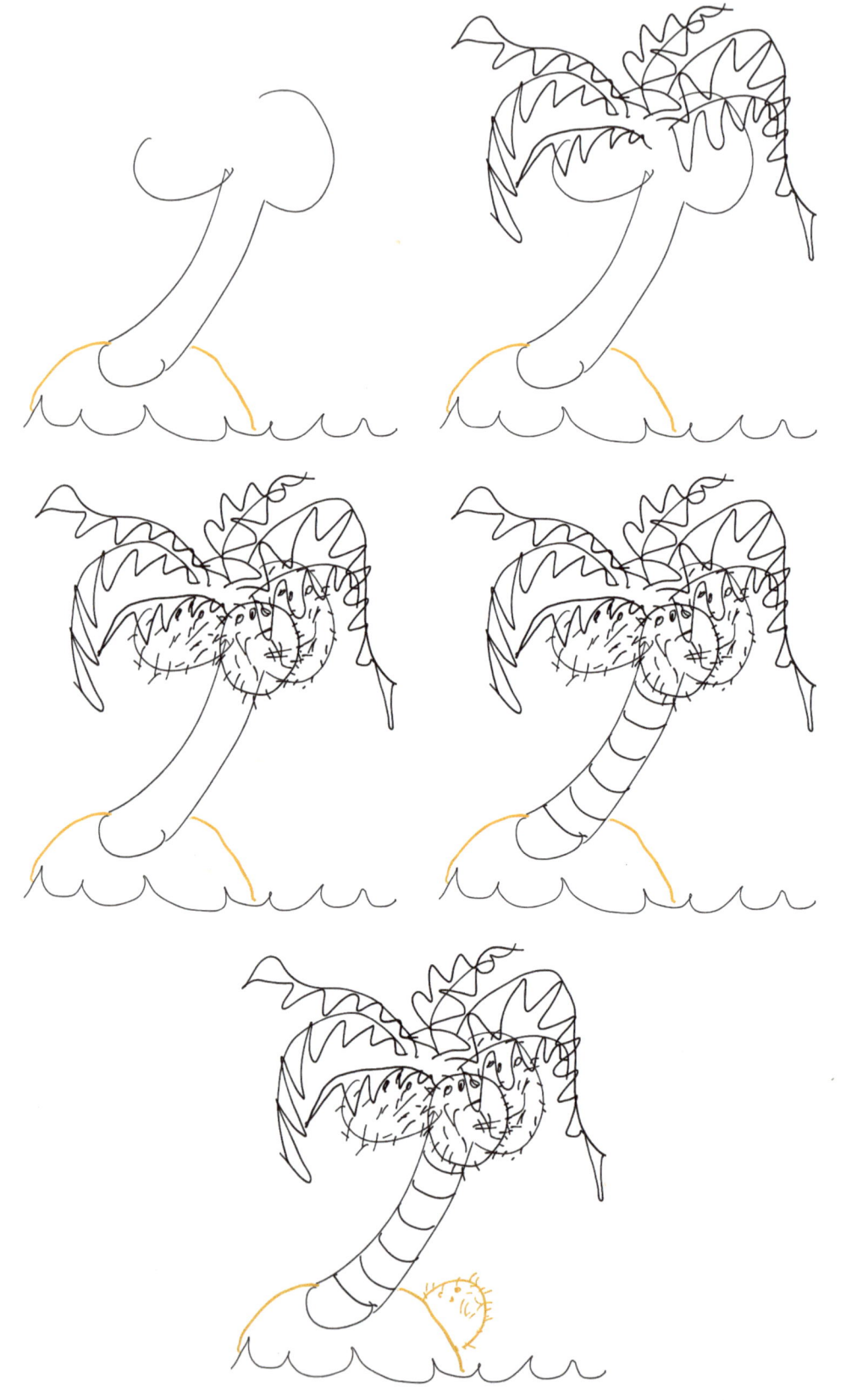

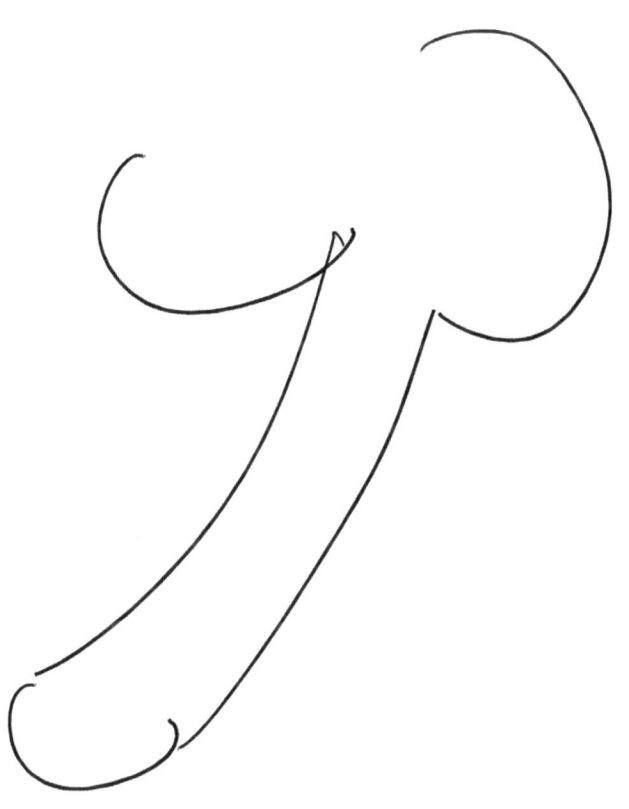

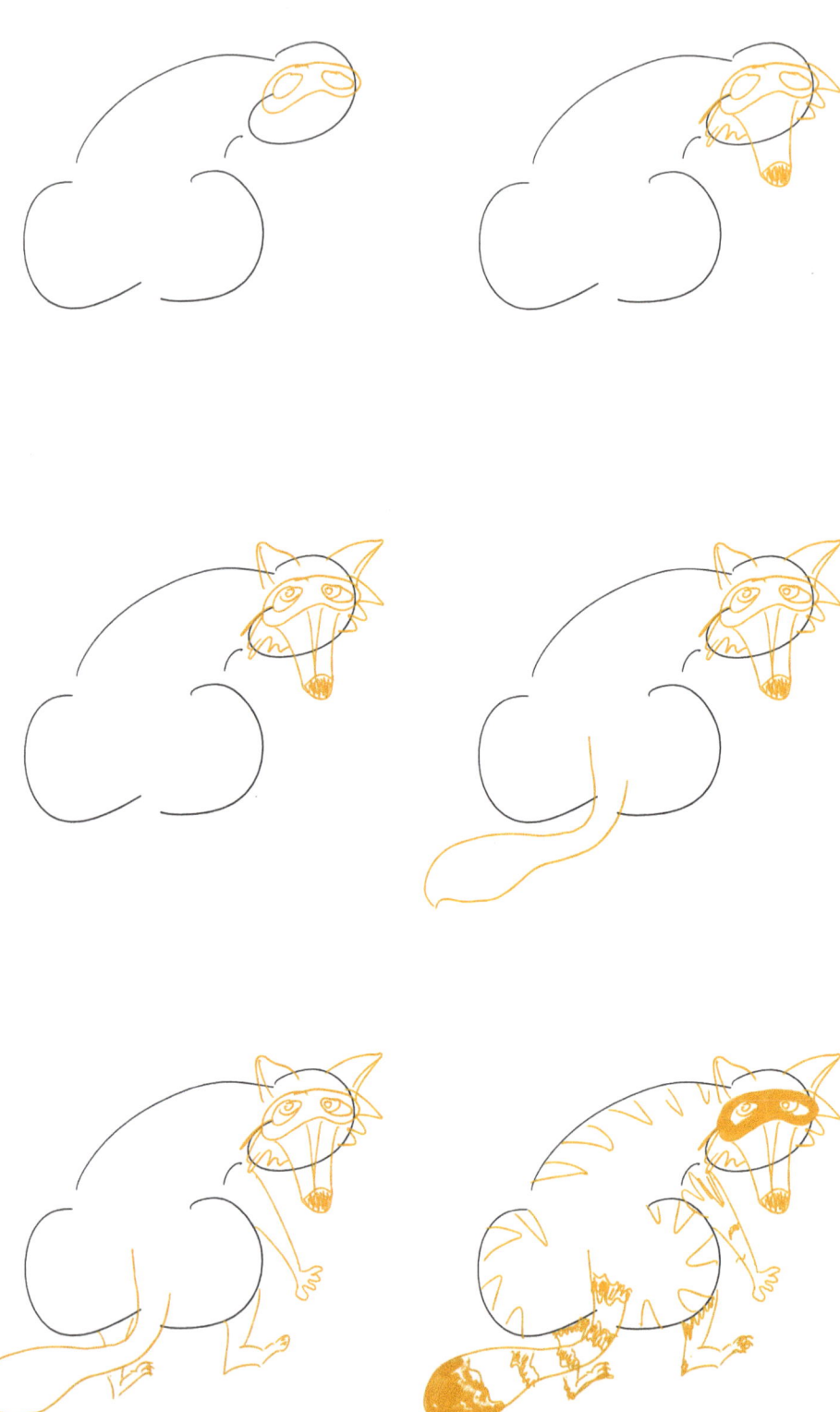

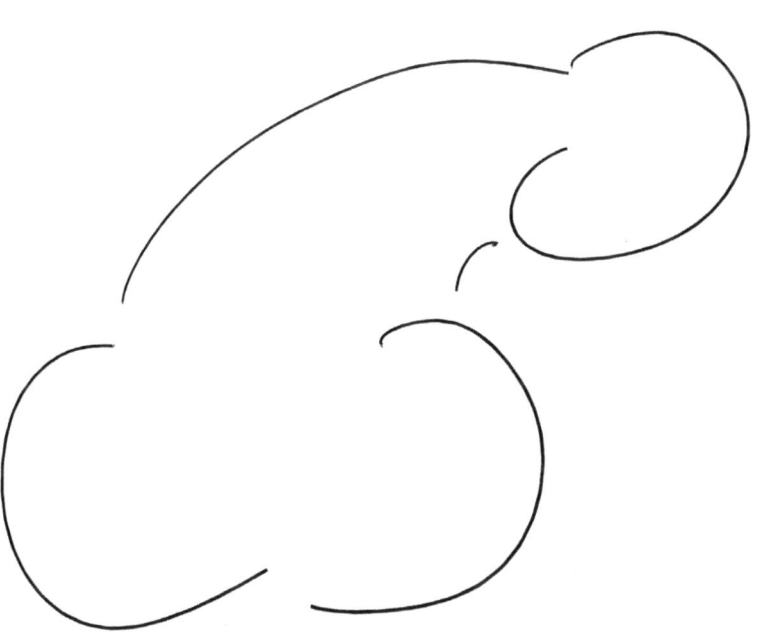

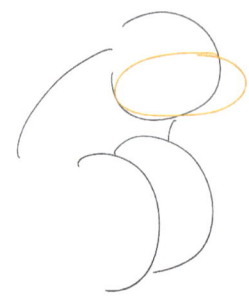
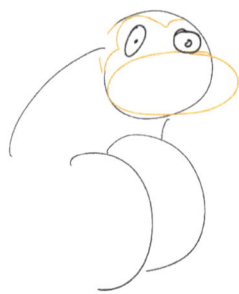
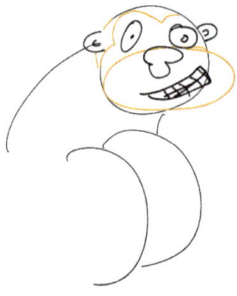
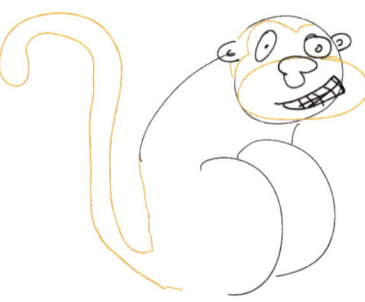
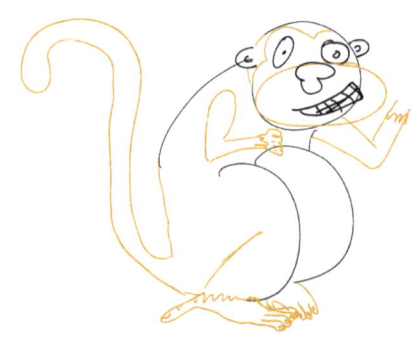
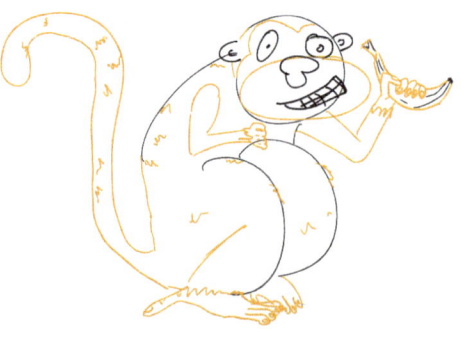

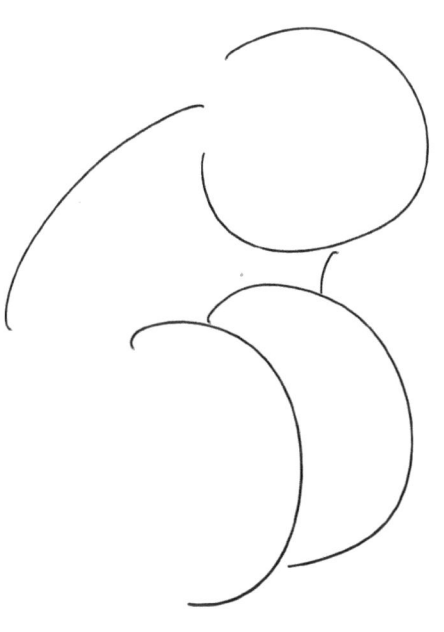

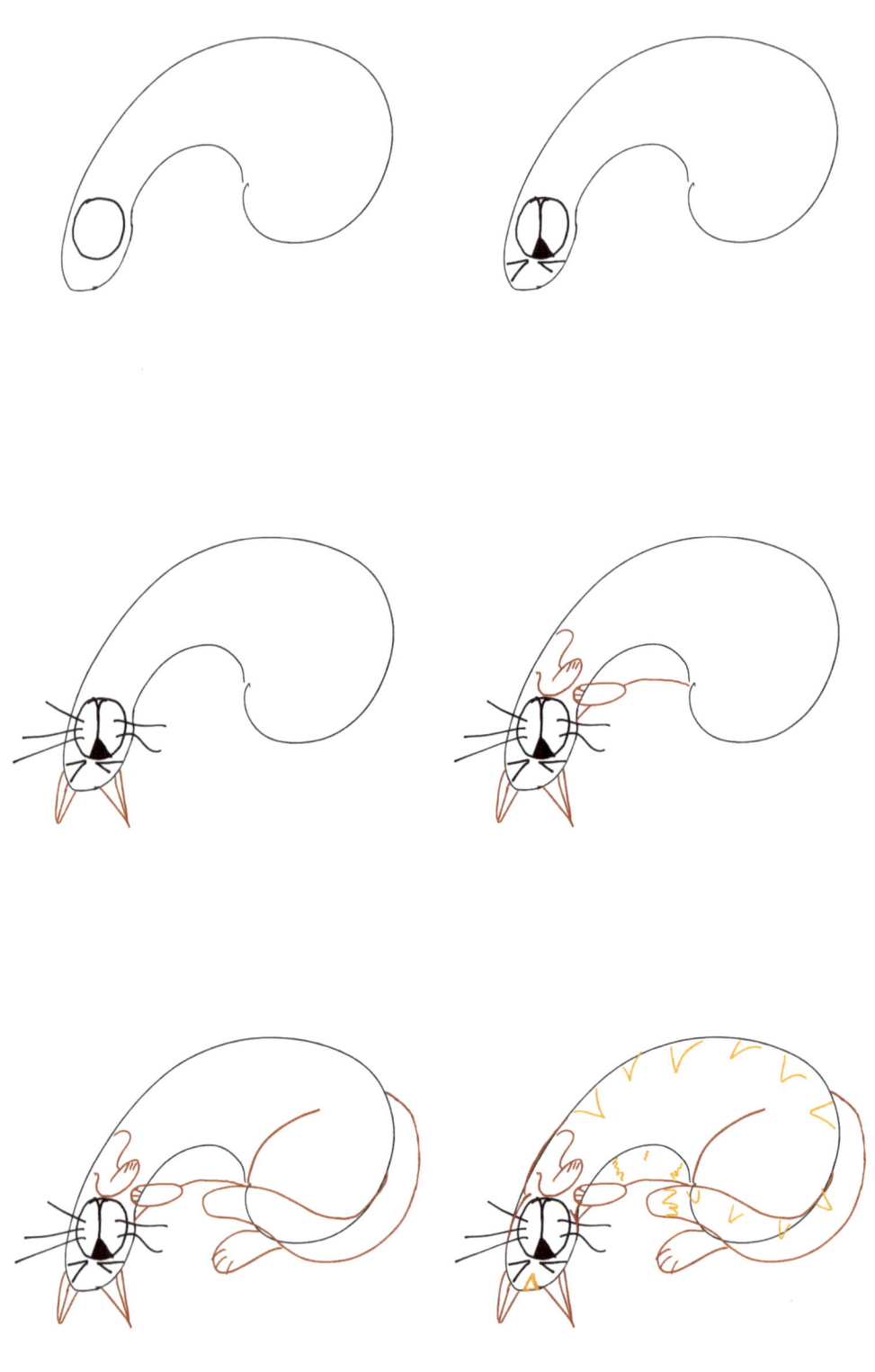

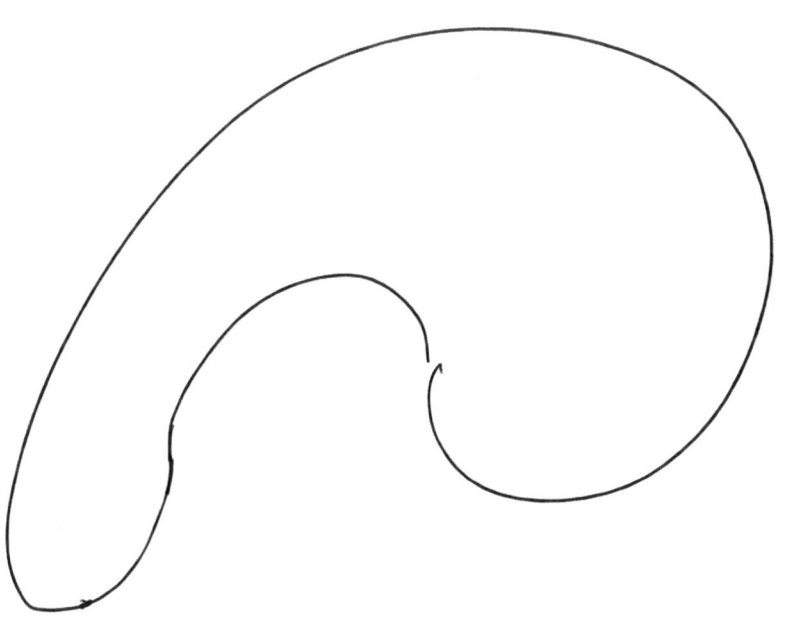

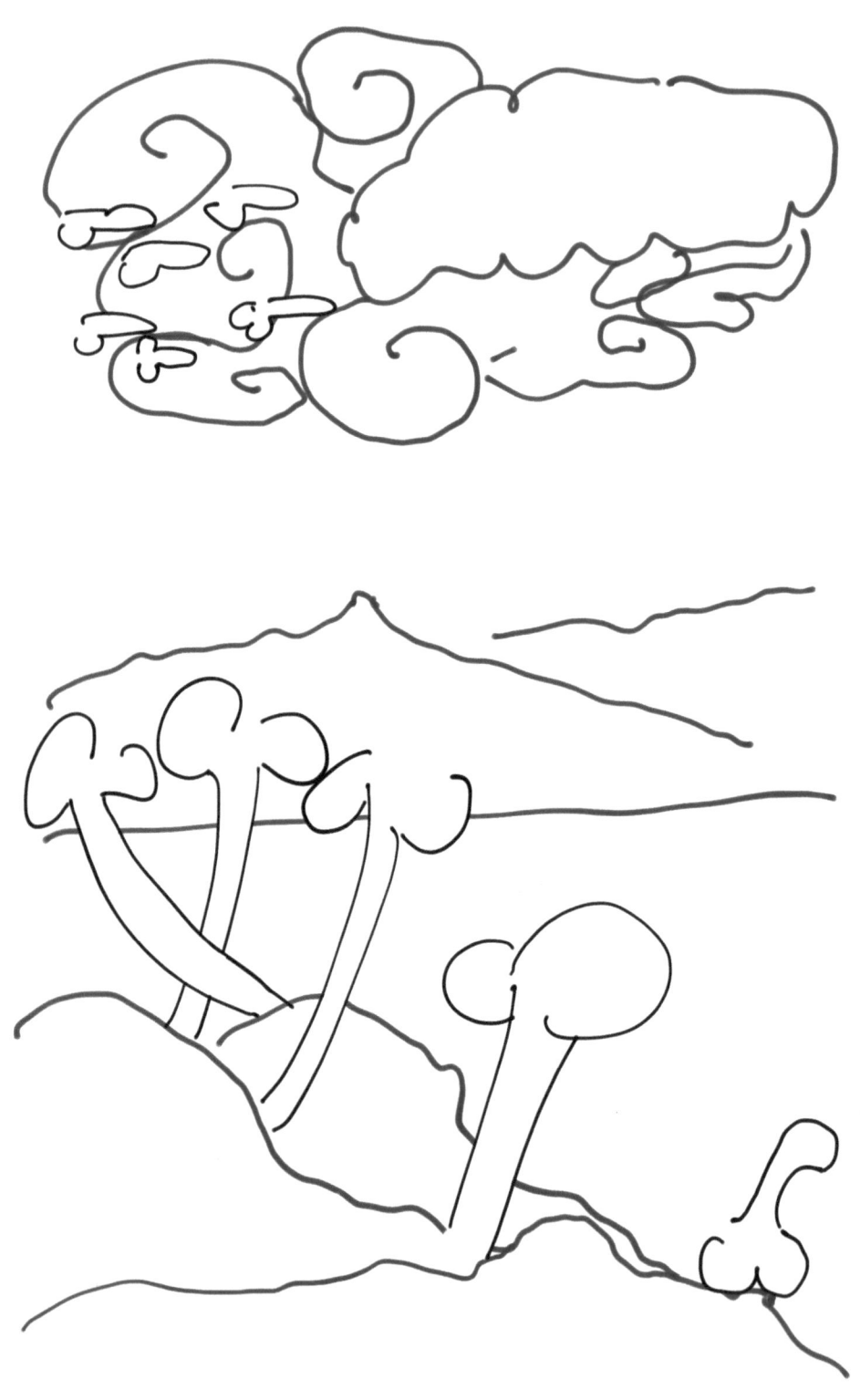

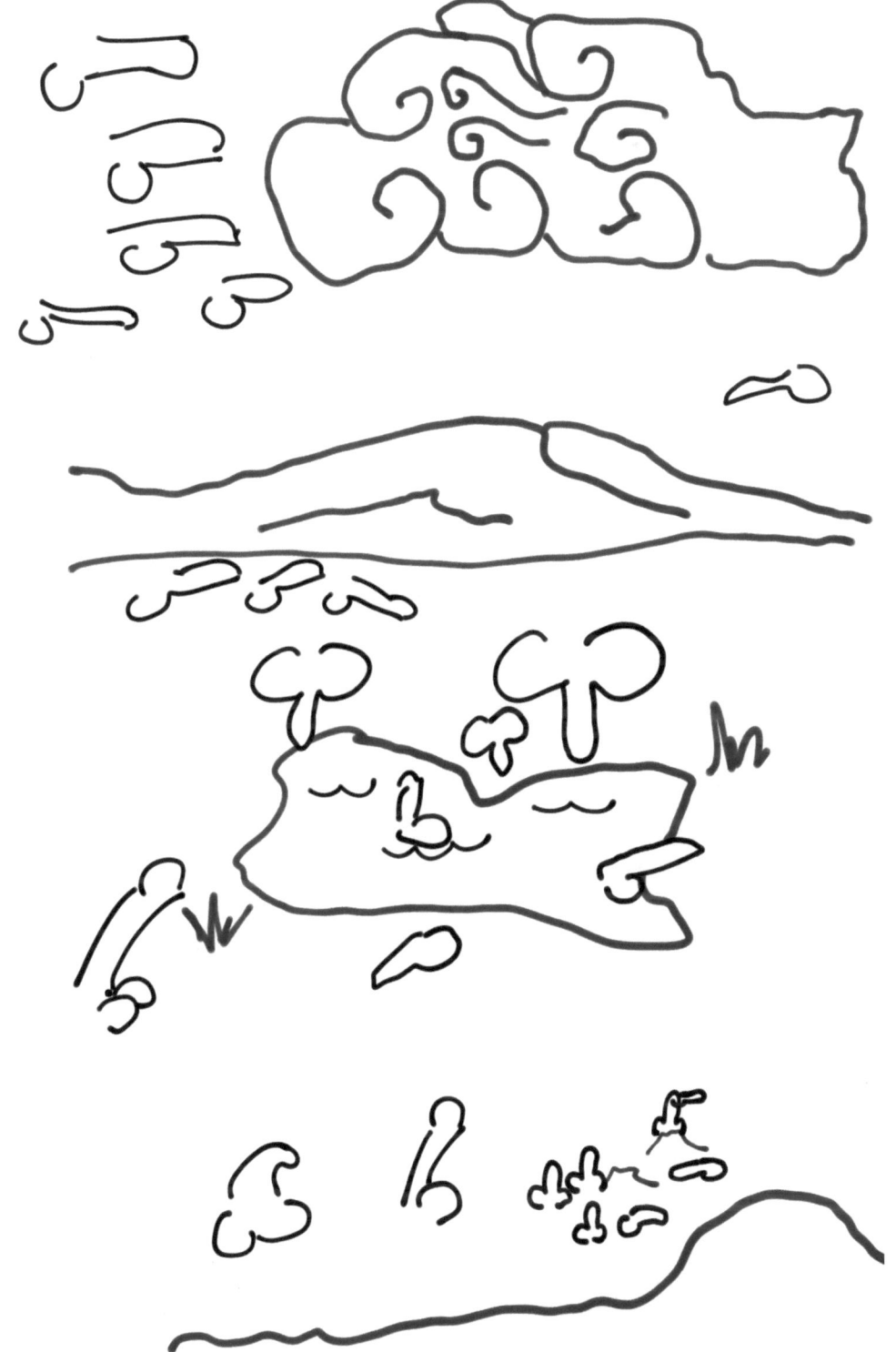

www.ingramcontent.com/pod-product-compliance
Lightning Source LLC
Chambersburg PA
CBHW040340220526
45473CB00009B/2741